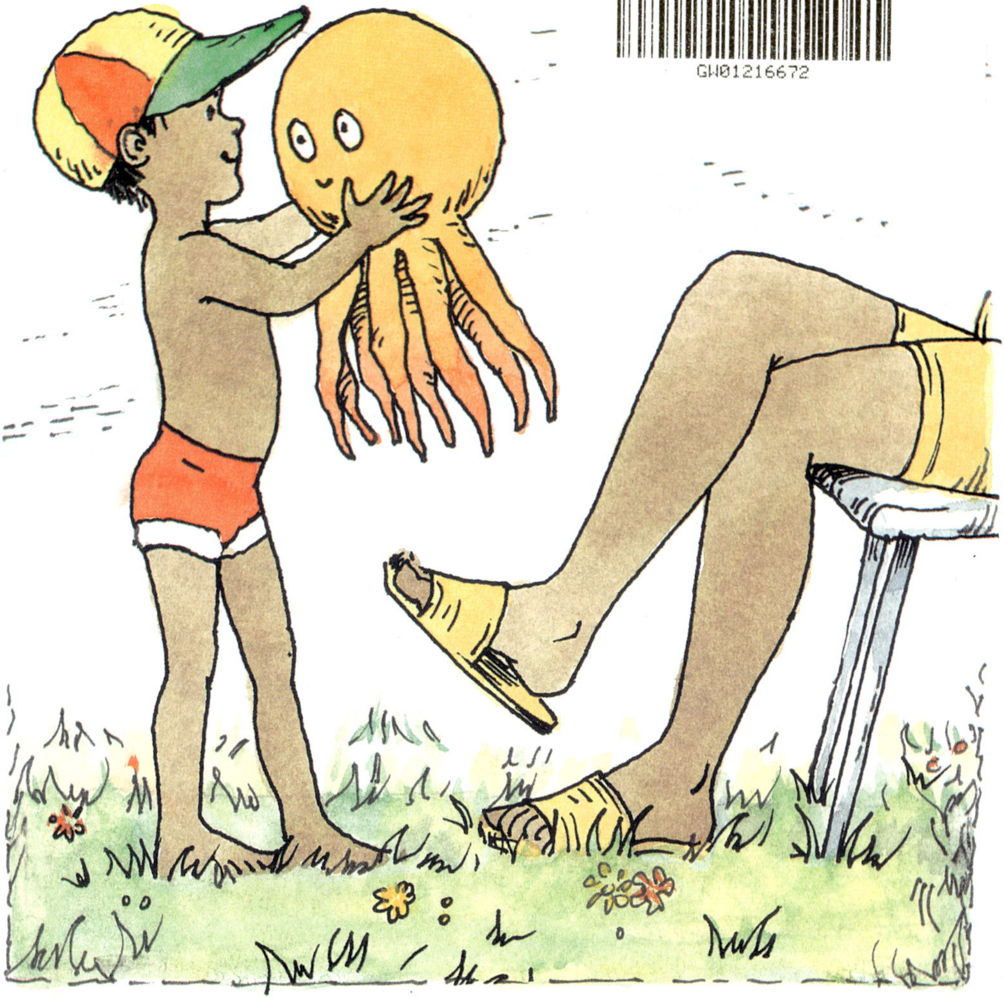

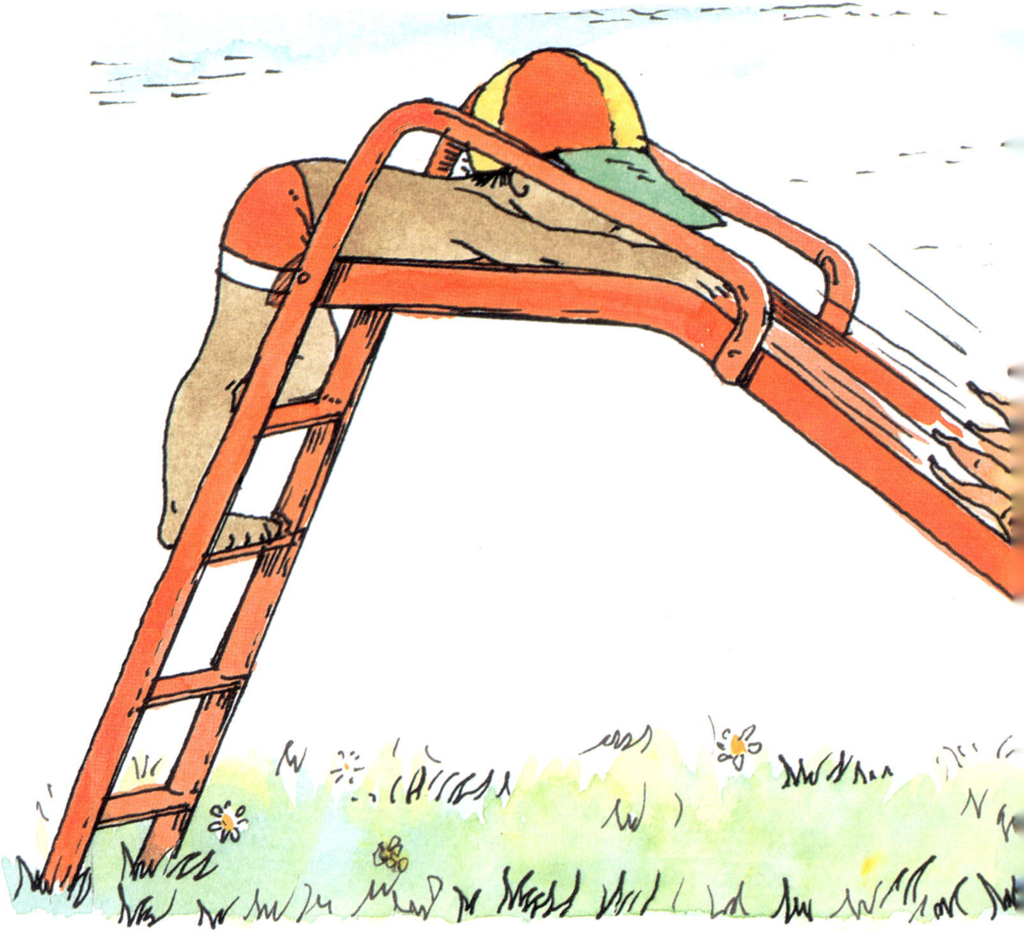

You like sliding

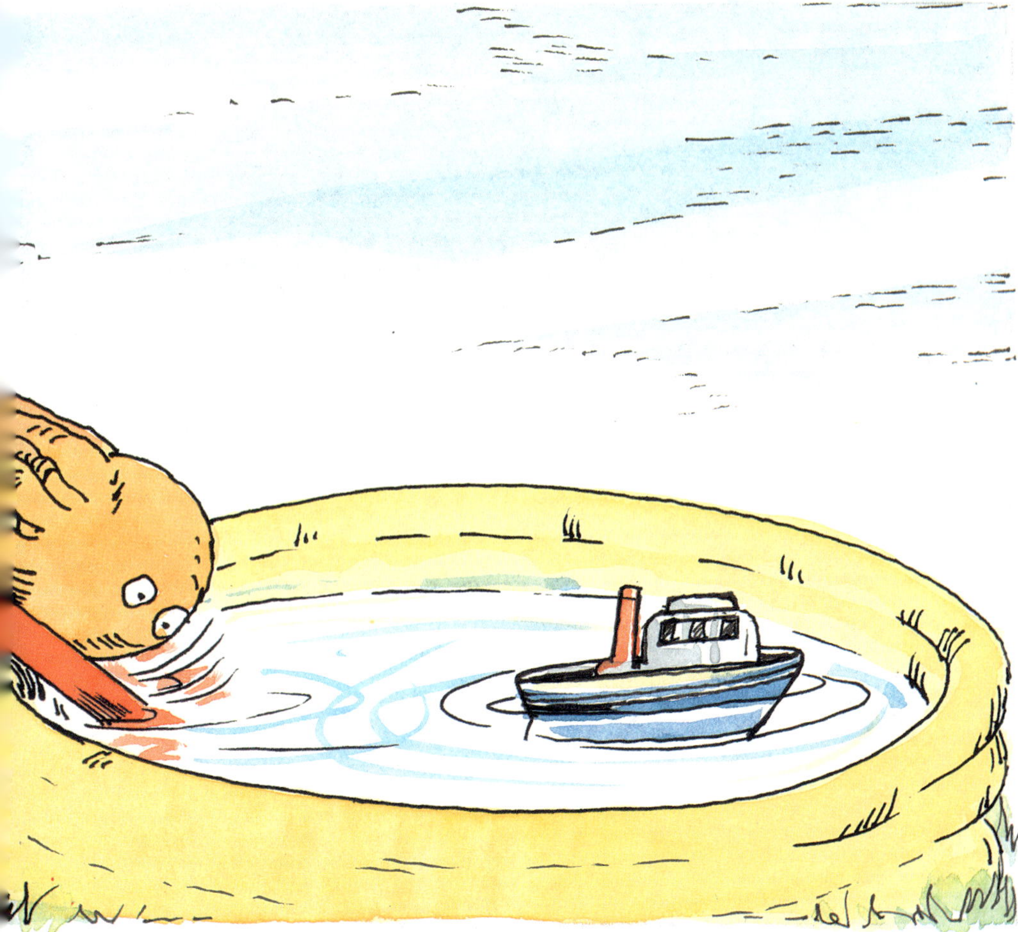

into the pool.

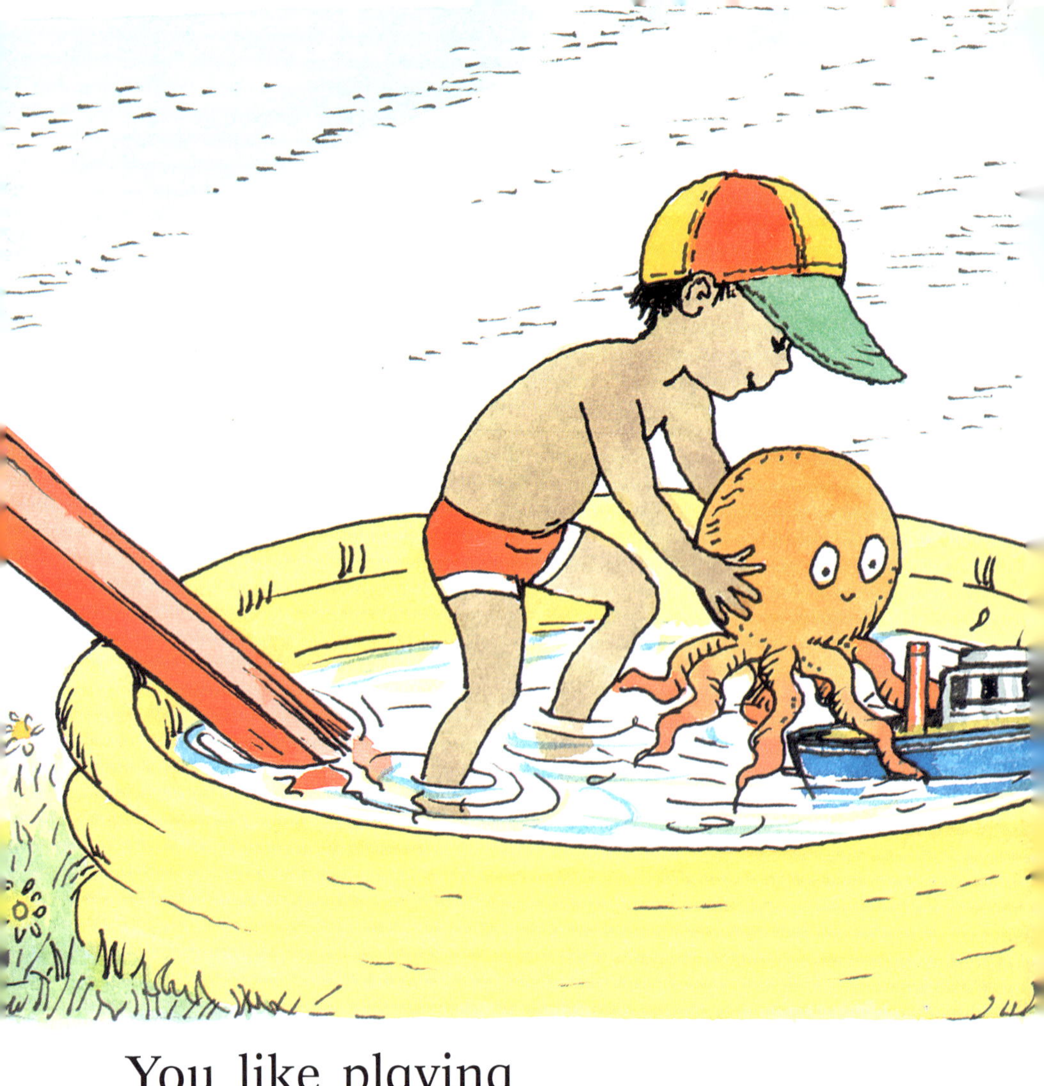

You like playing

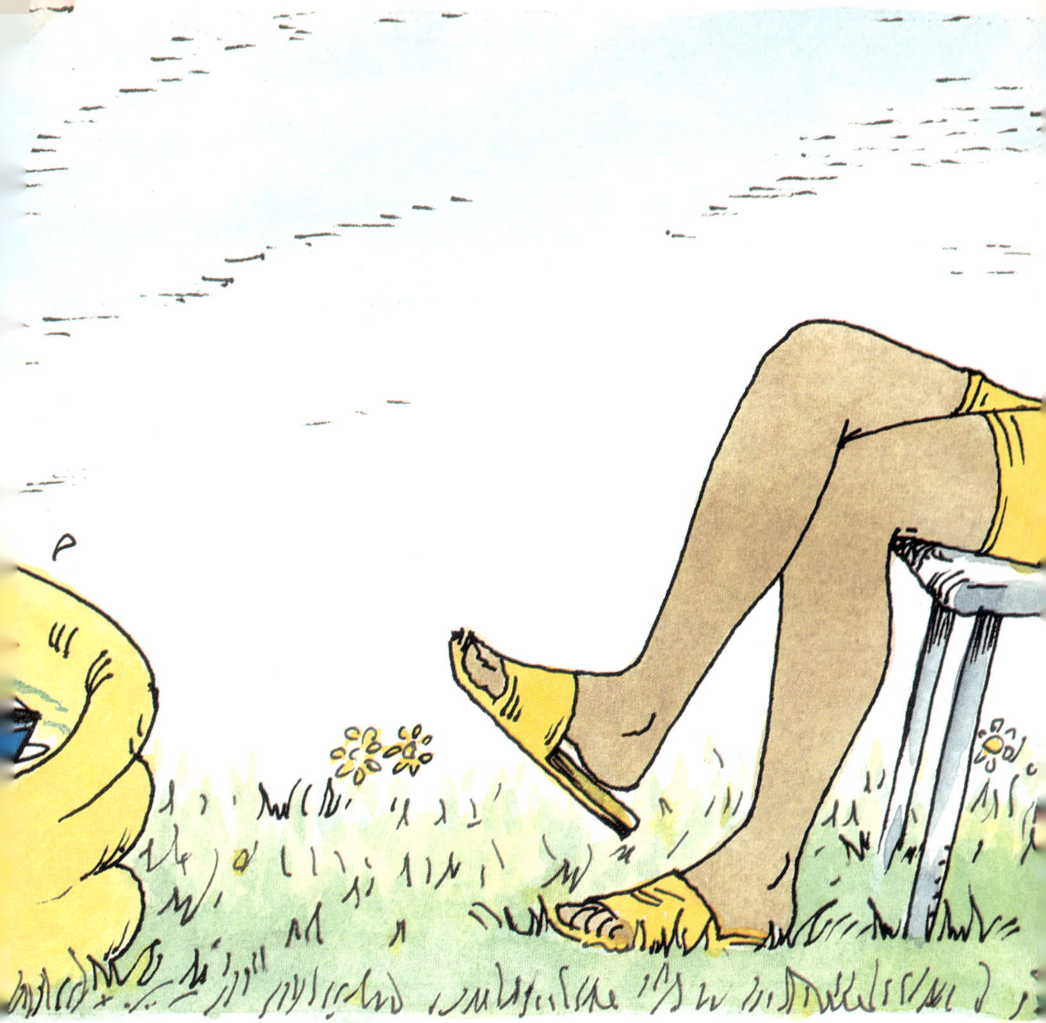

in the pool.

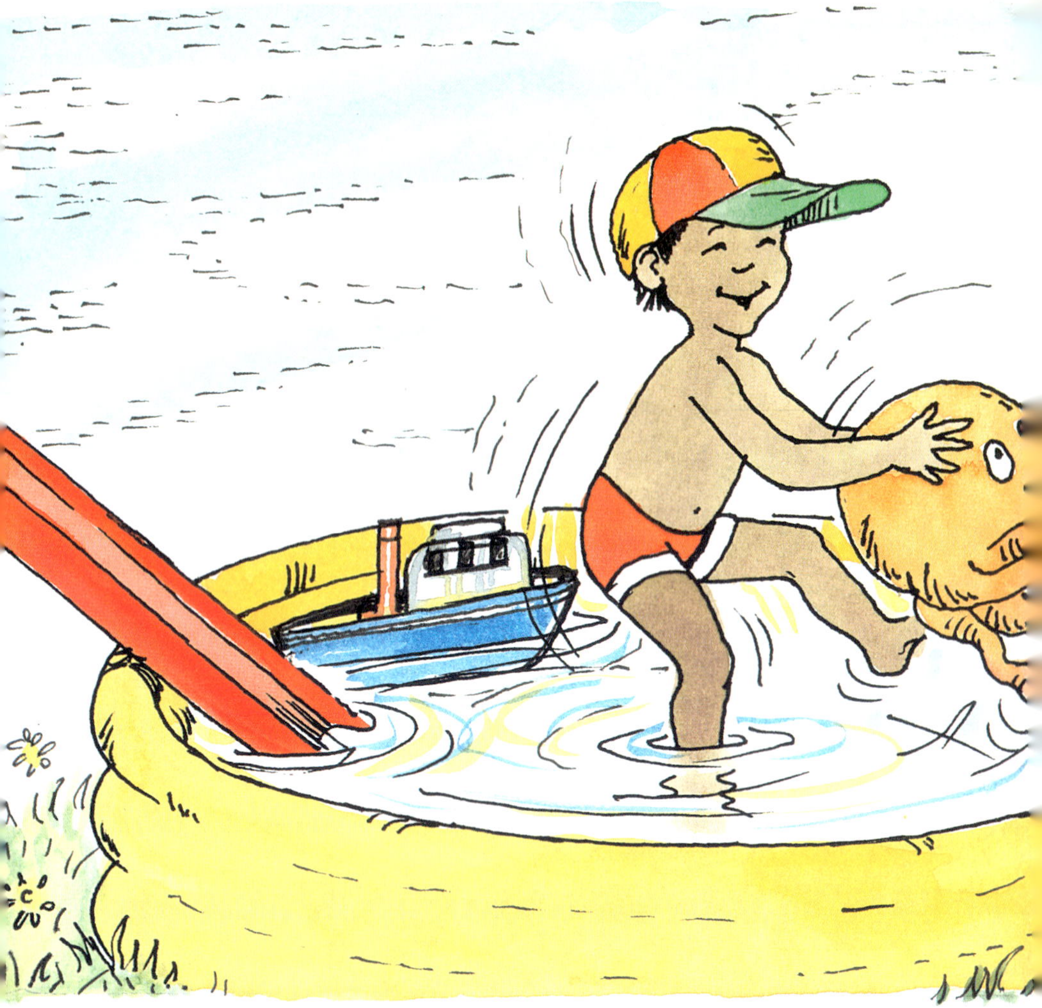

You like splashing

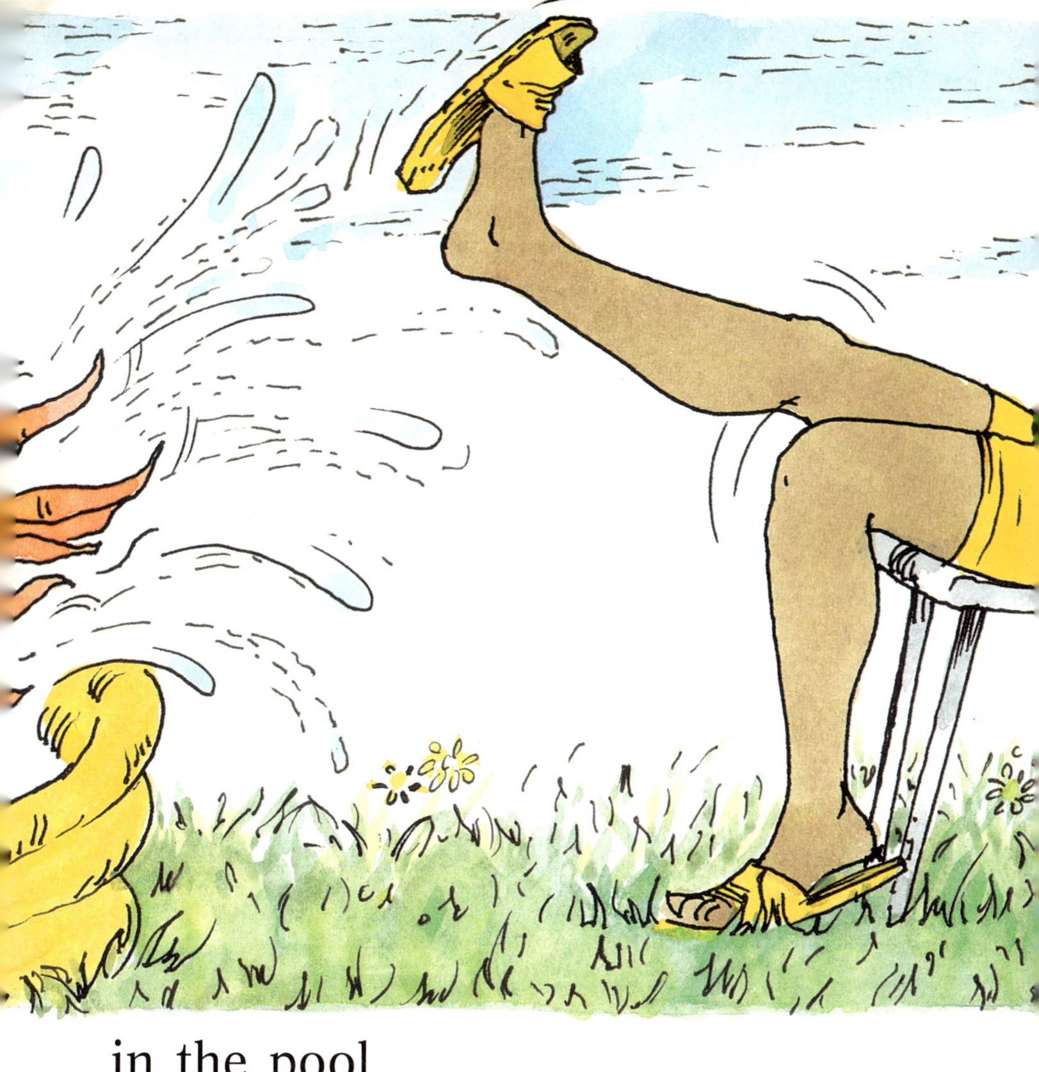

in the pool.

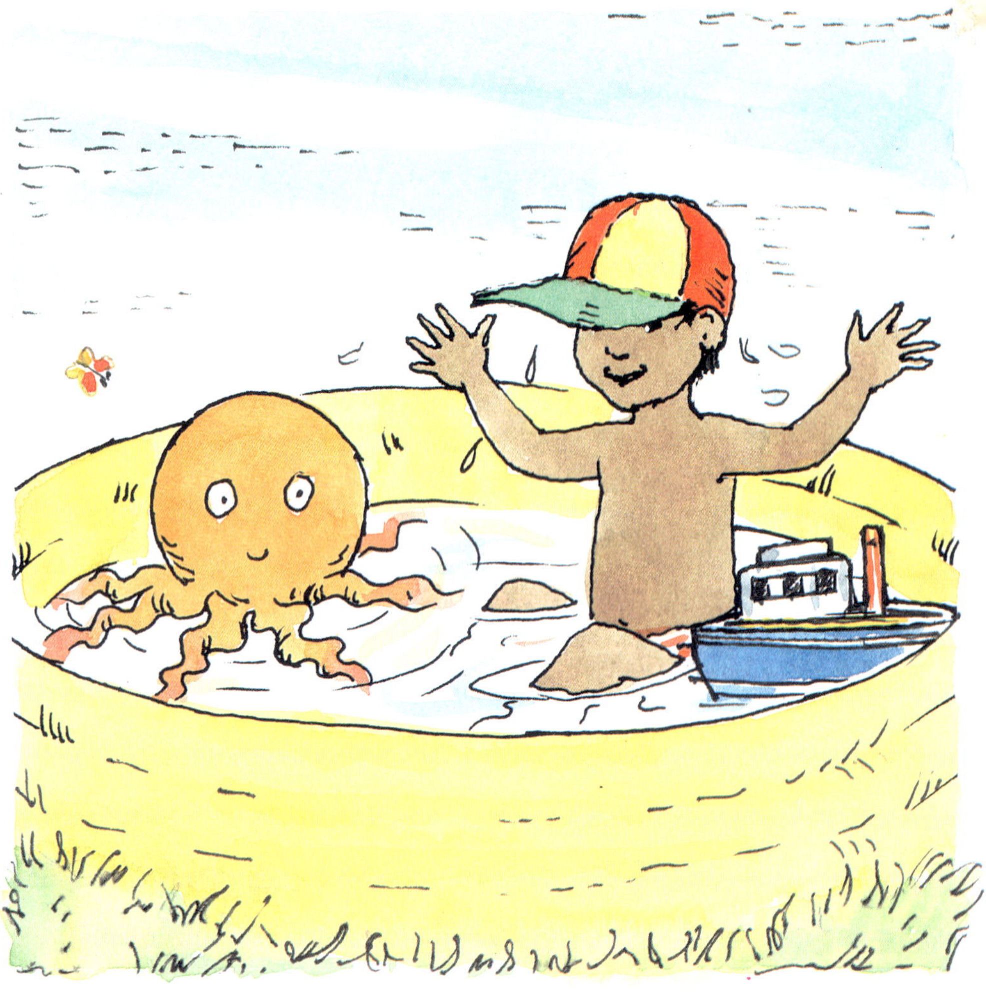

You like the pool!